CACTUS GROWING

FOR BEGINNERS

By

VERA HIGGINS, M.A., V.M.H.

LONDON
BLANDFORD PRESS

First Edition	*1935*
Reprinted	*1937*
Second Edition	*1943*
Reprinted	*1947*
Reprinted	*1950*
Reprinted	*1952*
Reprinted	*1953*
Reprinted	*1955*
Reprinted	*1956*
Reprinted	*1957*
Revised Edition	*1964*
Revised Edition	*1971*
Reprinted	*1974*

ISBN 7137 0128 5

ACKNOWLEDGEMENT

The colour illustrations were photographed by Edgar and Brian Lamb in the Exotic Collection at 16 Franklin Road, Worthing, Sussex

Printed by A. Wheaton & Co., Exeter

CONTENTS

ILLUSTRATIONS

The line-drawings on pages 8, 11 and 33 were drawn by the author.

FOREWORD TO 1971 REVISED EDITION

FOR many years Mrs. Higgins was one of the foremost growers of succulents in the country and her methods of cultivation achieved success. Thus few changes in the text were needed to bring her instructions in line with modern ideas. However, the names used in the earlier editions were those in use in the first quarter of the century. In recent years there has been a spate of name changing, a process which is still continuing. Names have therefore been changed to those in most general use today as some of the names given in the earlier editions are no longer to be found in catalogues or books. Even so, plants may be offered under several names although those now used in the text will be recognised by all nurseries.

R. GINNS

CHAPTER I

INTRODUCTORY

To the general public, anything spiny is a cactus, but botanically the name cactus is reserved for members of the family Cactaceae. The plant with fleshy pointed leaves, commonly known as the Partridge-Breasted Aloe, is not a cactus. Actually it belongs to the same family as the Lily. Then there are plants rather larger than Aloes, also with thick, fleshy leaves, armed with sharp teeth, that are sometimes seen in tubs or even out-of-doors in the milder parts of the country; these are Agaves, and whereas the Aloes are chiefly found in Africa, the Agaves all come originally from America. These belong to the same family as the Amaryllis.

There are also other families in which some of the members are succulent; in Euphorbiaceae, which includes the Sun Spurge of our woodlands, there is a large succulent section which is found in Madagascar, the Canary Islands and Tropical Africa, but the most interesting species come from South Africa. These have so well adapted themselves to their dry surroundings that some of them with their very thick swollen stems hardly look like plants at all. Some of these have spines and look very much like cacti; but the flowers are different. Other succulents found in collections include Gasterias and Haworthias, belonging to the same family as the Lily; Cotyledons and Echeverias of the family Crassulaceae, and that very interesting group, the Mesembryanthemums, from South Africa. The 'mimicry' plants belong to this family, so called because their swollen leaves joined closely together resemble, in shape and colouring, the pebbles and rocks among which they grow.

The true cactus belongs to a very large family which is found only in America though it is very widely spread in that continent. A few members of the family bear leaves and have woody stems, but the majority have very small leaves which soon fall off, or none at all, and the stems are green so that they may do the work usually performed by leaves. In nearly all cases, cacti have spines; these spines vary very much in size, form and colour but always spring from a small cushion known as an areole; the presence of the areole is typical of cacti; it it usually woolly when young but may become bare with age. Other plants, such as Euphorbias, do not have areoles as their spines arise in a different manner and are structurally different.

The succulent cacti vary very much in shape; some of them are columnar and may, in their native place, grow to as much as sixty feet almost unbranched, like the Giant Cereus, which is the State Flower of Arizona. Others are more barrel-shaped and it is said that some of these are used by travellers in the desert as a source of water; if the top is sliced off and the inner flesh crushed, quite a fair supply of liquid is obtained, which is practically tasteless and quite harmless.

Many of the desert cacti are quite small, either spherical or more elongated; sometimes they grow singly, sometimes together forming large 'cushions'.

With the exception of one or two extreme forms, such as the 'Dumpling Cactus' which contains a bitter narcotic, and some of the Ariocarpus, which closely resemble the rocks amongst which they live, almost all the desert cacti are characterised by their spines. These vary in form and may be needle-like or stout, very short or several inches in length, straight or with the tip hooked, and the colour varies from pure white through all shades of yellow, red, brown to black. For each species the type and number of the spines in each areole is generally constant and this forms an important characteristic in identifying the plants. It should be remembered that under cultivation spines tend to become weaker and less highly coloured, especially if the atmosphere is too moist or the plant grown too fast.

Despite the popular fallacy that cacti do not flower, well-grown plants of many species will produce blooms regularly in this country. In their native haunts the flowering of the cacti may be a wonderful sight; it generally occurs at the beginning of the growing season and when the weather is propitious it is no uncommon sight to find whole acres covered with sheets of brilliantly coloured blossoms, with their satiny petals widespread to the sun. Many cacti have pink or magenta flowers, others are yellow, orange and scarlet; those which flower at night are usually white and sometimes sweetly scented. In some species, the flowers open for several days in succession but others open once only and then perhaps for a few hours at most. Those which open at night are generally over by the next day, though the Echinopses, which generally open in the late afternoon, may remain open (without closing at night) for several days.

The flowers are succeeded by fruits which may be dry and almost hidden in the wool till they split and release their seeds, or they may be fleshy berries, often scarlet and very attractive to the birds. The Mammillarias have rather small flowers but borne in considerable numbers, in a wreath round the crown of the plant; these are followed by scarlet berries which usually take a year to develop so that

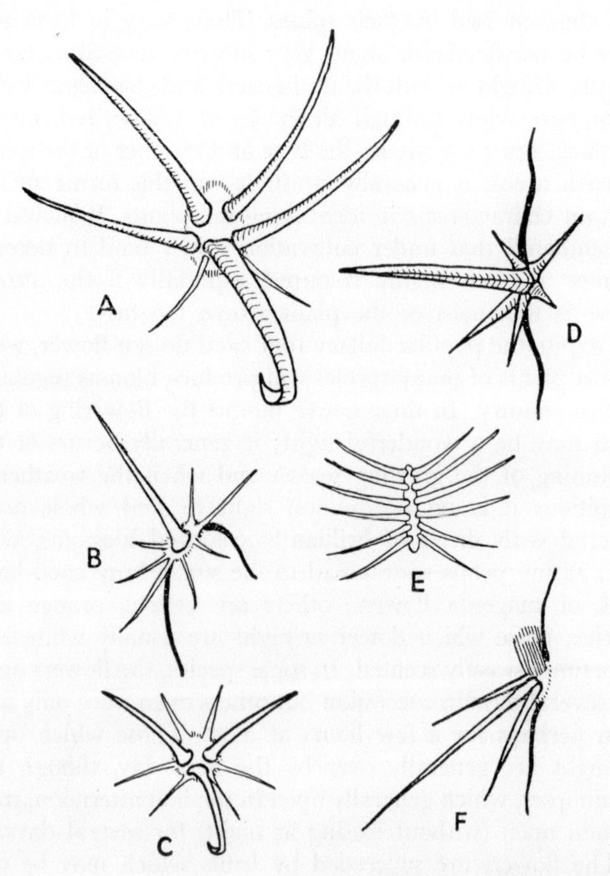

Drawn by V. Higgin

Fig. 1. Types of Spines.

A. Echinocatus.
B. Mammillaria.
C. Echinocactus.
D. Cereus.
E. Echinocereus.
F. Opuntia.

plants may be seen bearing rings of flowers with rings of scarlet fruits below. Large flowers, such as those of the Echinocacti, produce large fruit, as big as cherries or walnuts. Most cactus fruits are edible in the sense that they are not poisonous, but not all are pleasant. Opuntia fruits are eaten largely by the natives and are offered for sale in the markets; so are some of the Mammillaria berries, which taste like strawberries; in fact, a few produced even in this country can scent the greenhouse when they first appear, the scent being variously described as like pineapple or fruit salad.

We have been speaking mostly of cacti which grow in the open desert under extreme conditions of drought, under a burning sun; there are, however, a few types, generally considered to be less highly developed and nearer their original ancestors, which are found in moister places such as the tropical forests of Central America; these plants do not need to be so much protected from drought as the air is never dry, and the spines are not usually much developed. Most of these cacti do not grow on the ground where the soil is very wet and stagnant, but on the trunks of trees and the stems are long and slender, climbing or trailing. These cacti have very beautiful flowers, some of the night-flowering species having the largest blooms in the family, up to ten or twelve inches across. They are sometimes grown trained over the roof of a greenhouse and will, when old enough, produce a good number of their lovely blossoms.

One of the difficulties encountered by the beginner is the nomenclature, which at first sounds rather difficult but with familiarity soon becomes intelligible. Every plant is given two names, the generic name which comes first and is always spelt with a capital letter, and the specific name, which may be an adjective describing the plant or the name of the discoverer, or the place in which it grows. This name, nowadays, is always spent with a small initial letter. Both names may be in Greek or more usually in Latin or a latinised form. This should not be difficult to follow for, after all, we each have at least two names, a surname and a Christian name; the generic name of a plant may be likened to our surname, while the specific name corresponds to our Christian name but, for plants, they are used in the reverse order. Plants are grouped together in accordance with their relationships to one another. Thus two plants which resemble each other in all particulars are said to belong to the same species, and they then have the same specific name. Those which resemble each other in some important particulars but not in all are said to belong to the same genus and have the same generic name, but different specific names.

The cactus family is divided into three sub-families, each of which is again subdivided. The older classification of Schumann recognised only 21 genera but the standard classification of Britton and Rose (1919–1923) recognised 124 genera. Since that time the number of genera has been considerably increased by workers in various countries, partly by splitting up the old genera and partly on account of the new plants recently discovered. One of the latest classifications by Backeberg, 1958, names 220 genera although some of these are not generally recognised. The modern tendency is to reduce the number of genera. The names listed in catalogues may vary and sometimes the generic name is followed by another in brackets which indicates that both these names have been given to the same genus, thus: *Chamaecereus (Cereus) silvestrii* indicates that the plant was originally regarded as a *Cereus* but the more generally accepted name now is *Chamaecereus.*

The total number of species of cacti known is very large, and though a few species have never been imported into

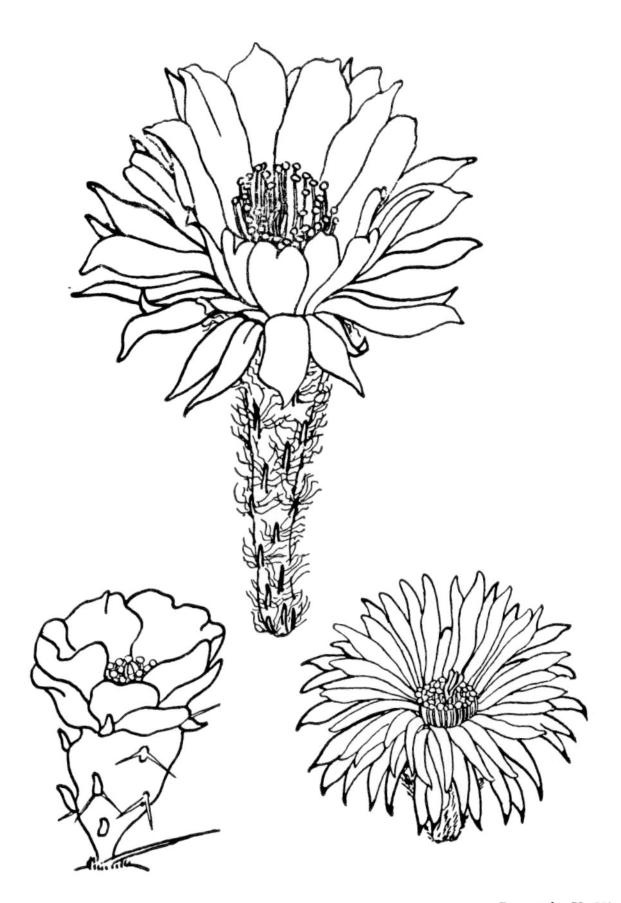

Drawn by V. Higgins

Fig. 2. Types of Flower.

Echinopsis.

Opuntia. Echinocactus.

Europe, specimens of the great majority are to be found in collections in the Old World. The beginner therefore should not be discouraged if he cannot immediately name all the plants in his possession. The naming of plants from photographs and illustrations should be done very carefully as there are many pitfalls; often the scale is not given and a totally wrong impression may be gained by anyone unfamiliar with the subject of the picture; an Echinocactus which is really a foot across may, in a reduced photograph, appear to be quite a small plant. The help of a more experienced grower is the best way of beginning, but experience is the only real guide. It should not be difficult to place the plants in their genera in quite a short time, but the addition of the correct specific names is by no means so easy, especially in those groups where many species closely resemble each other.

It is as well to have all plants labelled; if the name seems unnecessary when a few plants are first acquired, it will generally be found later on that it helps in the understanding of the requirements of the different kinds of cacti and also when comparing one's plants with those of other growers. Wooden labels are rather clumsy for small pots and there are a number of better kinds made of celluloid, ivorine, etc., now available. The name of the plant should be clearly written in indelible ink or pencil. Some people like to keep a record of their plants, listing them on arrival and giving details of the source from which they were received and the date, together with any other information of interest. If the plants are numbered consecutively on arrival and the number put on the label in the pot, this makes an easy means of reference. By starting the list at 1,000 instead of 1, succeeding numbers have four figures which is a help in deciphering a partially illegible label.

CHAPTER 2

CULTIVATION

IN ORDER to grow cacti really well it is essential to have some knowledge of the conditions under which the plants grow naturally. Apart from a few varieties cacti grow where there is abundant sunshine. The majority live in the open desert or on high mountains; sometimes they are found amongst coarse grass, sometimes in loose sandy soil. The dry clean air of the desert blows over them, occasional torrential rain sinks rapidly through the porous soil, and is succeeded by long periods of drought when the only moisture available is from the dew. The roots spread out for a considerable distance, in the case of some Opuntias for several yards, close to the surface, so that advantage is taken of every drop of rain that falls.

Compare this with the conditions that our plants have to contend with. Long periods of sunshine are rare, more particularly in autumn, when it is most valuable for ripening off the plants, and in the winter. The value of such sun as we have is reduced by the fact that it passes through glass which diminishes the ultra-violet rays, while the tendency to scorch is increased. The atmosphere contains a large amount of moisture and, particularly near towns, is far removed from the purity of the desert air.

Of necessity we imprison our cacti in pots, and sooner or later we crowd the pots, and therefore the plants too, as close together as possible in order to make room for new arrivals.

On the other hand, cacti in their natural habitat often have a hard struggle for existence. They exist where non-succulent plants would perish, and sometimes bear evidence of the struggle. It is here that the cultivator at home has his chance. If the cactus asks for very little it is by no means averse to a more generous diet. It can go for many long months without moisture though it would be grateful for a little more. It will exist on the poorest of soils, but if it has the chance of a slightly richer one it will respond amazingly.

A word of warning must be put in here however. It is very easy to overdo liberality. It is not likely that you will kill a cactus from neglect though it will look miserable as the result of it, but it may be killed very quickly indeed by too much kindness.

The greater number of cacti are found in Mexico, Texas and Arizona in North America; and in Peru, Bolivia and Argentina in South America. While the temperature may be very high during the day, the nights are often cool, and in the Andes the cacti are sometimes covered with snow. In all these districts the rain is not only limited in amount but also occurs at more or less distinct periods, so that, except for dew, there is practically no water available to the plant either as rain or in the soil for several months on end. It is important to remember this dry period when growing cacti. The fact that the amount of soil available to each plant is very much less in amount than is natural means that what there is should not be too poor, or should be changed fairly often. This does not mean that what the nurseryman considers a 'rich' soil should be used; leaf mould or manure are dangerous to most cacti, but a good loam is advisable.

The very rapid drainage of desert soils should certainly be imitated as far as possible under cultivation.

The cacti which, as mentioned earlier, grow in damp forests may be given more generous treatment though the drainage should still be free, for in their natural conditions the roots are not in soil but run along the cracks in the bark and many of the roots are formed on the branches (aerial roots) and obtain moisture from the air. But there will be a certain amount of humus trapped in the bark so that peat may be added to the soil for plants of this type.

The chief requirements of cacti in cultivation are a porous soil, plenty of sun and fresh air, a reasonable temperature and the right amount of water *at the right time*. We will deal with these points in order.

CHAPTER 3

SOIL AND POTTING

THE question of the soil most suitable for cacti has been much discussed and various mixtures recommended through the years. At one time burnt clay was considered to be the best but this material is probably unobtainable now. One thing is certain – whatever type of soil is used it must be porous; the compost usually recommended consists of equal parts of good loam; coarse sand or broken brick and neutral peat. Most succulent plants like lime which can be added in the form of old mortar rubble but the epiphytic cacti which grow in damp forests, prefer an acid soil. [Editor's note: It is now generally considered that cacti prefer a slightly acid compost and that lime is definitely harmful to some genera such as Rebutias or Notocacti.] Leaf mould should not be used since it may contain spores of fungi. For growers who cannot easily mix their own compost the John Innes Compost No. 1 is recommended; this can be purchased in small quantities from most horticultural sundriesmen. Coarse sand should be added for the more succulent types.

The epiphytic cacti, which have flat green stems and few spines, do not want to be kept too dry and peat can be added to the soil.

The method of potting is of importance. Cacti will exist in very small pots, but they grow better if given reasonable

Plate I (*Opposite page*): MYRTILLOCACTUS GEOMETRIZANS

root room; the statement that they flower better if root-bound is open to doubt; most people who increase the size of the pot as the plant grows find they get flowers when the plant has reached a reasonable size. Constriction of the root, if persisted in, checks growth and dwarfs the plants.

The pots, which must bc absolutely clean, should measure at the top not less than the diameter of the plant, including the spines. The hole at the bottom of the pot should be large. This should be covered by a concave crock in the ordinary way, though some people prefer a piece of perforated zinc which prevents insects getting in. A good layer of broken brick or smaller crocks is then added so that there is good drainage.

When the plant is placed in position, with the roots spread out as much as possible, the compost should be filled in until the neck of the plant, in the case of a globular cactus, in completely covered. Deep planting is advisable as it encourages the formation of roots higher up. Half an inch of space should remain between the surface of the soil and the rim of the pot to allow for watering. It is not necessary to ram the soil down with force; just bump the pot a few times on the bench to settle the soil round the roots, holding the plant firmly during the process.

Water should be able to run through the compost freely; if it remains on the surface for any length of time, it shows that the mixture is not sufficiently porous.

The spines of cacti are not poisonous, but they are not pleasant things to get in the fingers. Leather gloves are useful for wear when potting, and if the plant is large and heavy, sheets of folded newspaper wrapped round the plants will help to make the handling easier.

Young cacti should be repotted each year but as they grow older every other year should be sufficient, depending

---

Plate II (*Opposite page*): NOTOCACTUS OTTONIS

on their rate of growth. Spring is the usual time, before the plants have been watered after their winter rest, in which case they should be kept dry until growth has started. Some experts repot during the growing season; our observations tend to show that this to some extent checks the flowers. Early spring would see to be the best time. All the old soil should be gently shaken clear of the roots, which should be trimmed back if unhealthy or broken. If the same pots are used they should be first scrubbed. Repotted at this time of the year, the compost should be fairly dry and no water given until the commencement of the growing season.

By courtesy of the Editor of "My Garden"

Fig. 3. ECHINOPSIS EYRIESII VAR. ROSEA.

CHAPTER 4

SUN AND VENTILATION

THE best place to grow cacti in Britain is in a greenhouse, or even a frame from which frost can be excluded during the winter months, but many people with small collections, especially in towns, are not able to have these convenient structures; they need not therefore be debarred from growing cacti as these plants will do quite well in a living room. They are best kept on the window sill where they will get most sun and air.

They may look very decorative on the mantelpiece, but, if there is a fire, this position will be rather hot and, in any case, is too dark. Small glass cases are sold for use in rooms. These have the advantage of keeping dust off the plants, but a second layer of glass between the plants and the sunlight tends to cut the latter down too much. When pots are stood on the window sill, they will probably be put in saucers; if so, it is important to see that water does not remain in the saucers after watering or the soil will get sour. It is a good plan to put small pebbles or granite chips in the saucers so that the water can drain through the pots properly.

When the owner becomes really interested and the collection grows, then a small greenhouse will be needed. If a greenhouse containing other plants is already available, the cacti can be kept at the drier, sunnier end; they do not need much heat in winter provided they are protected from frost. The house should be in a sunny position, with plenty of ventilation. Greenhouses are rather expensive nowadays but there is a wide choice of size and type; the materials of which they are built may be wood, which will need painting at intervals, or aluminium, which needs little attention. It is important that the glazing should be well done so that there are no drips. Most cacti prefer rain water and this can be collected by running guttering along under the eaves which can be lead into a tank inside the greenhouse, under the staging.

If a choice of positions is available, the house should be placed so that the ends point North and South; it should be well away from trees or walls so that the plants receive all the sun available. A span-roof is generally best, but a lean-to, constructed on the south side of a wall, can be used; the wall will tend to conserve heat and may be lime-washed to make it lighter, and, if tall or climbing plants are to be grown, it is a decided advantage to have the additional height; the staging on the other side can then be used for the plants in pots and they will there be in the sun for the greater part of the day.

Special attention should be paid to the staging, which should be covered with corrugated iron, asbestos board or some similar material, which, in turn, is covered with shingle, granite chips or coarse sand, as this allows free drainage of water from the pots. It also has the additional advantage of preventing draughts up through the staging and, if the heating apparatus is below, the hot, dry air rising from the pipes will not strike the plants directly. A strip of wood must be nailed along the outer edge of the stage to prevent the chips or shell from falling off. Along the west and north sides a narrow shelf may be run, six inches below the roof span, to accommodate the seedlings which will be all the better for being placed near the glass. In this position, the shelf will cast no shadow on the plants below during the major part of the day.

The pots should not be too close together; it should be possible to get at any plant without disturbing its fellows. As a matter of fact, the beginner will discover before very long that this is a council of perfection. As plant is added to plant the staging will not expand to keep pace; the pots will come closer and closer until they are touching; new shelves will be added in every possible and impossible position, until the only thing left is to get another greenhouse. Once the cactus has taken root in your soul it will spread like the Opuntia in Australia!

Although in this country we very seldom get too much sun, in very hot spells in the summer a little shading from the midday sun is good for the seedlings. Apart from this, assist the sun to get at your plants by keeping the glass clean. Near towns it is astonishing how soon a film of soot settles down, and even in the country it is rare to see really clean glass. If you think your glass is clean just damp your finger and rub it across a pane of glass and see what happens. If the roof can be reached easily, warm soapy water is the best means of cleaning it; in any case, friction must be applied and most roofs can be cleaned by rubbing with a long-handled broom or mop. It is no good trusting to rain to do the work; the film of soot is greasy and can only be removed by rubbing. Every autumn and spring the glass should be cleaned inside as well. If there are gutters feeding a rain water tank, it is as well to disconnect the feed to the tank while the roof is being washed, otherwise dirty water (and soap, if used) will foul the water in the tank.

Cleanliness is far above godliness in the successful management of cacti. Rubbish should not be allowed to collect under the staging and the floor, whether of ash or concrete, should be kept clean.

Next in importance to sun is fresh air. The top lights may be kept open day and night during warm weather; during the winter the ventilators should be opened in the daytime whenever the weather is dry, but in a fog, especially near a town, it is best to keep all the ventilators closed.

CHAPTER 5

HEATING AND WATERING

Cacti grown in a living room must accept the temperature at which the room is kept; during winter when there is a fire, the room may be as warm as 60–65°F. (15–18°C.) or more; this is really too hot for cacti at this time of the year, as it tends to make them grow, but the window sill will probably be cooler than the centre of the room and so is the best place to put the plants.

At night when the fire goes out, the temperature will drop considerably; this will do no harm provided there is no actual frost, and plants on the window sill are unlikely to suffer if curtains or a blind are drawn over the window at night.

In the greenhouse, where the temperature can be controlled, there is no necessity to maintain much heat during the winter months. It is far better not to coddle the plants. Frost should be excluded; 40–45°F. (4–7°C.) will keep all the plants safe, particularly if they are dry. Some of the Cerei like a slightly higher temperature, but will not hurt without it.

In very severe spells further protection can be afforded the plants if sheets of newspaper are laid over them. If the thermometer inside the greenhouse should register a degree or two of frost during the night, leave the newspaper over the plants, more particularly if the sun is shining next morning.

For large greenhouses the usual and the cheapest method of heating is by means of water pipes connected to a coke or anthracite stove. The fuel used will depend on the conditions. Large stoves run easily on coke which is the cheaper fuel, but small stoves are often easier to handle with anthracite, which burns more slowly and evenly in small quantities than coke does. The increase in cost is not great and generally worth while if the owner has to do his own stoking.

Unless the house is to be kept very warm, it is usually sufficient to have the pipes along one side (the cooler); but if the initial expense is no great object, a greater length of piping will be found more satisfactory as the required temperature in the house can be maintained with the pipes at a low temperature and in consequence they do not dry the air too much. A very short length of pipe is not easy to manage as, if the fire burns fiercely, the water tends to boil, and should the fire go out, the pipes will cool quickly.

Many amateurs with small houses find an oil lamp quite satisfactory; much the best kind is the lamp that burns with a blue flame and is surrounded with a water jacket, as it is economical in use and does not give off objectionable fumes. Some types offered are provided with flues to conduct the products of combustion outside the house; this is safer for the plants, but as a good deal of heat is lost this way, they are more expensive to run. Oil lamps must be kept scrupulously clean or the fumes will damage the plants. The chief danger in their use is if the wick is not properly adjusted and, in consequence, smokes; most users have this experience *once* and are ever after extremely careful, for the oily soot is very difficult to remove from the glass and woodwork, more difficult to remove from the plants themselves and, if it does no actual damage, spoils for a considerable time the beauty of species with white hairs or farina.

In districts where electricity is cheap, this affords a clean and easy method of heating and is especially useful to a busy owner who looks after the house himself and has not much time to spare on the daily, dirty business of stoking a fire or cleaning a lamp. The electric heaters used in dwelling houses are of a suitable type but these should either be specially wound or an adequate length of heater pipe used so that they are not run at too high a temperature. As used in dwelling houses, they are generally too hot for greenhouse work; it should be possible to touch the pipes, when full on, with the bare hand. The great advantage of this method of heating is that a thermostat can be installed which will automatically switch the current on or off as required; if the thermostat is set at 50°F. (10°C.), the switch cuts out when the temperature rises about two degrees above 50°F. (10°C.) and switches on again if it falls about two degrees below. A sudden drop in the outside temperature at any time is dealt with automatically and, once set going, such an electric installation will work for years without any attention whatever. With any other form of heating, the person in charge has to consider weather changes and stoke accordingly – not always an easy matter to the inexperienced.

Watering is one of the greatest stumbling blocks to the novice and it is not much help to be told that 'experience is the best master' if the process of learning results in the death of favourite plants. The ordinary non-succulent greenhouse plant, with its numerous stalks and leaves has the greatest possible area, not only for absorbing moisture, but for giving it out again. It cannot store up water; consequently as soon as the soil or atmosphere becomes too dry the plant wilts and will very soon die if not supplied with water.

But cacti are constructed to withstand extreme drought, and they do this by storing up water in their tissues to be drawn upon during the long rainless period to which they are subjected under natural conditions. They are for the most part leafless and the surface area through which moisture is evaporated is reduced to a minimum.

In their natural habitat, during certain parts of the year cacti get a fair amount of moisture, often in the form of heavy rain. During the rest of the time, and for considerable periods on end, no rain falls. Our object then is to imitate as far as possible the conditions of nature.

Cacti all come from America, but are so widely distributed over the Continent that their growing seasons actually occur at quite different times; they are however able to accommodate themselves to the British climate, growing in spring and summer and resting during the winter months.

Since over-watering is much more likely to cause damage during cold rather than in warm weather, it is best to keep the plants dry during the winter and to give more water when they begin to grow. Watering may commence about the middle of April if the weather is mild. Once a week is sufficient until signs of new growth appear when increasing amounts may be given until in really hot weather in June and July water may be given daily. Always allow the soil to dry out before giving fresh water, and then give plenty. As soon as August comes watering should be reduced to twice a week, and in September to once a week. Reducing the water supply before the growing season is over at the end of September enables the plants to ripen, which means better flowers the following year. From October until the following April, generally speaking, the drier the plants are kept the safer; this is more particularly the case if the plants are required to withstand a low temperature.

One's judgment must be exercised, but, generally speaking, Mammillarias and other globular desert cacti should be kept entirely dry. Some of the tall-growing Opuntias may show signs of flagging and a good drink once a month will revive them. The Epiphyllums and Rhipsales should be given a little water during the winter.

Plants in a room where the atmosphere is drier and warmer than in the greenhouse may need some water. A slight shrivelling of the plant is natural during the period of rest, it simply means that it is falling back on its own reserves of water, but there is no point in allowing this to carry on too far.

Even during the growing season the soil should never be allowed to become waterlogged. Cacti are accustomed to a very porous soil in their native land and the roots need air circulating round them as much as they need water. If all the spaces between the grains of soil are filled with water there is no air present and the roots may rot. The surface soil should be stirred frequently as this enables the roots to get air.

Do not be persuaded to ornament the surface of the soil with granite chips or other materials different from the compost. You may easily be misled into thinking the soil underneath is dry, whereas it may be sodden.

The can used for watering should be on the small side with a long tapering spout. Care should be taken to direct the stream on the soil and not over the plant. Water remaining on the plant, especially in a depressed crown, will act as a burning glass and damage the growing centre. Rain water, when available, is preferable to tap water; the chill should always be taken off before use, in summer by leaving it in the sun, in winter by adding hot water.

Syringing the plants with a fine spray is beneficial, as

it helps to keep them clean. This is best limited to hot evenings after sundown during May, June and July.

Finally, if in any doubt as to whether a plant needs water, it is wisest to withhold it. Damage is rarely done by under-watering, whereas over-watering is deadly.

Photo by R. Gorbold

Fig. 4. Opuntia salmiana.

CHAPTER 6

SEED RAISING

RAISING plants from seed is at once the most profitable and most interesting part of cactus culture. Certain Opuntias and Cerei grow rapidly and may grow to as much as six inches high in a year; but for the most part five to six years will elapse before the plant is mature, though it will often flower when younger. A well-grown seedling is a perfect gem, and is generally much more shapely than an imported plant.

Seeds may be sown at any time of the year if heat is available, otherwise sowing should take place from April to July. Fresh seed germinates freely, ninety per cent. being not unusual.

If several different kinds of cacti are to be raised from seed, they may be planted in rows in one large pan or each kind separately in individual pots. In either case, the pan or pots should be sunk to the rim in a wooden box containing peat which is kept moist. It is sometimes recommended to keep the temperature at 70°F. (21°C.). This may result in rapid germination but the resulting seedlings will be tender and, unless the heat is reduced gradually, may be difficult to deal with later. On the whole it is more satisfactory to aim at a temperature of 50–55°F. (10–13°C.) which can usually be maintained by putting the box in a warm position over the heating pipes and covering it with glass which

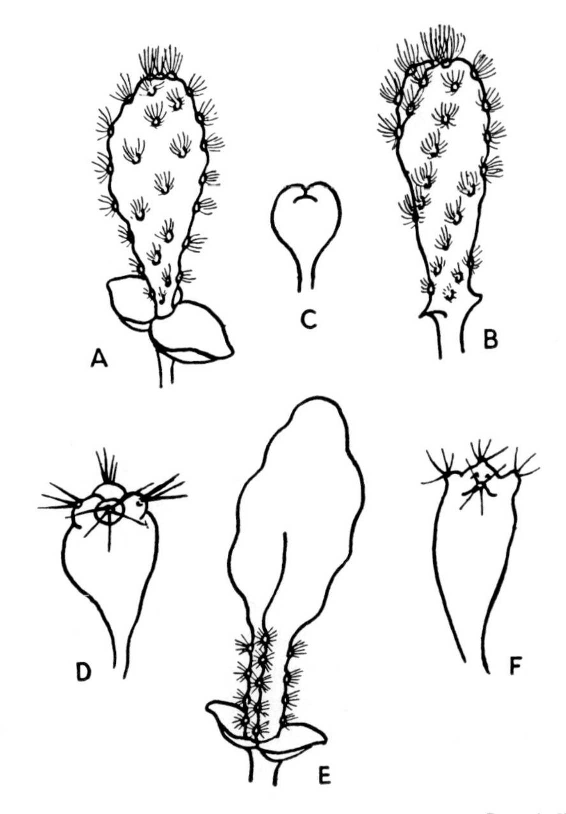

Drawn by V. Higgins

Fig. 5. Types of Seedlings.

A. Opuntia.

B. Cereus.

C. Echinocactus (just germinated).

D. Echinocactus (2 months old).

E. Epiphyllum.

F. Mammillaria.

should be turned and wiped if water condenses on it. Newspaper may be put over the glass which should be lifted later along one side to admit air until the seedlings are large enough for it to be dispensed with altogether.

The pots or pan should have a good layer of coarse drainage at the bottom and then be filled with the usual potting compost recommended for adult plants, the top inch being of the same compost passed through a fine sieve. It is advisable to soak the pots before sowing the seeds and to pack them into the wet peat; in this way, little or no watering will be needed until germination has begun. The seeds should be sown as evenly as possible and only the larger ones need covering with a thin layer of fine soil. Care should be taken, especially where several kinds are sown near each other, that they are clearly labelled.

Seedlings of cacti are not easy to handle and may die if squeezed or otherwise damaged. Any that have grown to a reasonable size can be pricked out two or three months after germination; they are best put, several together rather than singly, in a small pot. If, however, the surface of the soil is in good condition, with no moss growing on it, they can be left until the following spring when they will be stronger and will stand the move better; they should be given a little water during the winter and not dried completely as the adult plants are. They can then go singly into small pots, if large enough.

Plate III (*Opposite page*): ASTROPHYTUM MYRIOSTIGMA

CHAPTER 7

CUTTINGS AND GRAFTS

MANY cacti may easily be reproduced from cuttings; in some cases joints may be broken off and rooted; in others part of the stem or side branches may be cut off and used for propagation. Cuttings taken during the growing season root readily. The cut should be a clean one without jagged edges; after separation it should not be planted immediately but left to one side to dry. A small cutting may be placed in the soil the following day, a larger one after two or three days. The soil on which the cutting is placed should be fine. It may consist of either pure silver sand or a mixture of sand and sifted peat. The bottom of the pot should contain the drainage material as described in the chapter on soil and potting.

Should the cutting be of any length or be top heavy, a support should be tied to it, projecting two or three inches below the cut. This serves to keep it steady in the soil. The soil in which the cutting is placed should be slightly damp, then place the pot in the shade giving no water for a week or ten days, and then sparingly until rooting has taken place. Instead of using a separate pot for each cutting, many people keep a box filled with sand in which a number of cuttings can be placed when required and removed as soon as rooted.

The best, and indeed the only, time to take cuttings is

Plate IV (*Opposite page*): WILCOXIA POSELGERI

during the months of May to August, unless there is some means of giving bottom heat, when they may be taken at any time.

Some cacti are exceedingly prolific in offshoots. The question arises whether it is better to remove these and so allow the parent stem to receive all the nourishment it can, or to allow them to grow at will. When the plant is valuable and of use for purposes of exchange one or more of the offshoots may be taken off and rooted. Sometimes the original stem is ugly and battered looking, in which case it is better to remove the offshoots and grow them separately.

When offshoots spring from the base of the plant, obviously the natural way is for them to grow in clusters, *Trichocereus schickendantzii* for example, and very often they make their own roots and take on growth independently of the parent stem. Plants with this kind of growth should be allowed to grow naturally, for a good cluster is a pleasing sight. The button cactus *(Epithelantha micromeris)* forms a beautiful cluster and so do many of the Mammillarias.

Where the offshoots grow out at various angles from the middle or upper segments of the parent, it is wiser to remove most of them. This applies especially to Echinopses which are particularly prolific in offshoots; if allowed to remain in any number these will hinder the development of flowers.

Cacti may also be grafted; this method is used if a plant does not grow easily on its own roots and also, since grafted plants often grow more quickly, by dealers as a means of rapid propagation. It should be remembered that grafted plants are unnatural and may not be true to type.

Grafting is not particularly difficult and the beginner may like to experiment if he has suitable plants available.

Some strong growing stock such as a Cereus or Opuntia is chosen, the top is cut off and the plant to be grafted cut so that the surface area of the two cuts is of similar size; they are then pressed together and lightly tied so that they cannot shift until union has taken place. Owing to their drooping habit Epiphyllums are often grafted on Pereskia stems so that their flowers may be seen to better advantage; in this case the thin, woody Pereskia stock is split longitudinally for a short distance and the leaf-like Epiphyllum stem inserted in the split and tied till the two have united.

CHAPTER 8

TYPES OF CACTI

The beginner should set himself to learn the main characteristics of the common genera that he is likely to meet with; only in this way is there any hope of identifying a plant. With few exceptions all that a beginner can hope to do is to place a plant in its correct genus; to identify the species will need help from an expert.

It is most interesting to note how, as a collection grows, the different plants will fall into definite groups having similar characteristics. The subject will be dealt with as simply as possible here; for a fuller and more scientific treatment the reader is referred to more advanced books.* The genera that the beginner is most likely to meet are Opuntia, Cereus, Echinocereus, Echinocactus, Echinopsis, Mammillaria and Epiphyllum.

Members of the Opuntia group are frequently met with as they are easy to grow and quick to propagate. The most usual types have flattened, fleshy, green stems sometimes as large as a dinner plate with little clusters of spines arranged symmetrically over them. Sometimes there are one or two large spines in each areole, sometimes many smaller ones; as described earlier, an areole is the small cushion on which the spines, etc., are borne and is typical of cacti. In

---

* *Cacti* by J. Borg, and the 4-volumed *Illustrated Reference on Cacti and Other Succulents* by Edgar and Brian Lamb (Blandford).

this Opuntia group, and in this group only, there occur in the areoles small stiff bristles known as glochids; these are loosely attached and come off very easily when the plant is handled; they are, moreover, barbed so that, though they enter the hand easily enough, they are very difficult to extract; they are not poisonous but can be very irritating and in consequence Opuntias should be carefully handled. If a number of glochids accidentally get on the hand they should be covered by a strip of adhesive plaster. When this is pulled off the glochids are removed with the plaster

The original genus Cereus is now divided into numerous genera although some of the plants still remain as Cereus. They are mainly tall columnar types with ribbed stems; on the ridges are the areoles which may be near together and contain a large number of spines, or be more distantly placed so that the green flesh shows between. Sometimes the green skin is covered with a waxy deposit which gives it a blue or greyish appearance. Some of the Selenicereus and Hylocereus, usually those with fewer ribs, are climbers and may be seen trained over the roof of a greenhouse. They do not, as a rule, flower until they are several years old, and the plants have attained a fair size, but the young seedlings or small cuttings are attractive and well worth growing. Cerei come from both temperate and tropical America; in Arizona the giant *Carnegia gigantea* grows to a height of 50 ft. or more and is a conspicuous feature in the landscape.

The group ECHINOCEREUS contains a number of species which may grow as single plants or in groups; the stems are elongated but do not reach any great height; they are ribbed and bear areoles along the ridges. In many of the species the areole is elongated and the spines arranged along the two sides like the teeth of a comb (pectinate); they are often flattened against the plant and may interlace so that

Photo by R. Gorbold

Fig. 6. ECHINOFOSSULOCACTUS.

very little of the green flesh is visible. The Echinocerei produce large flowers as a rule; these occur near the top of the plant and break through the skin above the areoles that are two or three years old. They have short tubes covered with bristles and the petals, often bright pink or purple, expand out horizontally. This group was at one time classed with the Cerei and the flowers, botanically, are very similar, but the growth of the plant is rather different and it is better to consider them as a separate genus. They are found chiefly in Mexico and the adjacent parts of North America, never in South America.

The original genus Echinocactus contains a very large number of plants and has been split up by Britton and Rose into 28 genera. As one becomes familiar with the various types one realises that these smaller groups are very definite and that the subdivision is fully warranted. The present genus Echinocactus contains only a few species known as Barrel Cacti in the U.S.A. owing to their shape and size. The new genera are all plants whose height is less than or does not greatly exceed the width; they are ribbed and sometimes the ribs are rounded and the areoles occur at intervals along the rounded edge; sometimes the ribs are narrower and the areoles may occur in indentations or on projections along the edge. All the true Echinocacti and the related Ferocacti which are commonly grown in collections attain a considerable size in their native habitat and these cannot be expected to flower in this country until they approach adult size, but others do not grow so big or are capable of flowering as quite young plants. The spines of many species are stout and long, sometimes several inches long, and curved towards the tip, while if you run your nail along the spine you will notice that in several of the species it is corrugated. The flowers may be any colour, white, yellow, pink, red and purple and all have short tubes and widespread petals.

ECHINOPSIS is a well-known genus, specimens of which are often seen in cottage windows. When young, the plants are pear-shaped with ten or twelve fairly sharp-edged ribs; the spines are short and stiff and not very numerous in each areole. Even when young the Echinopsis will produce flowers which are remarkable for their size and beauty; they come from areoles situated in the upper half of the plant and have no stalks but a very long flower-tube, often covered with hairs, and the petals spread out into a large cup, in the centre of which is a tassel of stamens. The expanded flower may be as much as six inches or more across in some species. The Echinopses all come from South America, and though the plants resemble some of the Echinocacti they can readily be distinguished when they flower by the length of the flower tube and by the short smooth spines.

One of the most popular genera and the easiest to grow are the MAMMILLARIAS. These plants are usually spherical, occasionally elongating with age and are easily distinguished from the other genera by the form of the plant body, for the ribs are divided up into definite tubercles, by which is meant a projection or nipple, arranged spirally round the plant and an areole is borne on the tip of each tubercle. The flowers are, on the whole, small but often make up for their size by the profusion with which they occur, forming in some cases a complete ring round the plant near the top, sometimes even two or three rings at the same time. The position of the flowers is unusual for they do not come from the areoles as with most other cacti, but from the depressions between the tubercles.

The fruits of Mammillarias are little red (occasionally

By courtesy of the Editor "My Garden"

Fig. 7. EPIPHYLLUM.

white) berries; they mature within the plant and are pushed out suddenly about a year after flowering, so that it is not unusual to see a Mammillaria with a crown of flowers bearing just below a second ring of red fruits. The reason for this delayed development is that the seeds are thus ripe when the rainy season occurs and are not scattered during the very dry period when they would not germinate. Mammillarias occur chiefly in Mexico and the adjoining States, but a few are found in the Northern part of South America, usually on high ground and not amongst the tropical vegetation.

The EPIPHYLLUM is a well-known plant seen in many greenhouses; it is quite different from all the preceding types. The branches are flat, even leaflike, sometimes three-winged, and are apt to become straggly, but the flowers are large, beautifully coloured and freely produced during late spring and early summer; some species flower only at night and some are sweet scented. Seedlings and young branches have spines which disappear in the adult plant.

CHAPTER 9

HOW TO MAKE A COLLECTION

THERE are many ways of acquiring a collection. Friends will help by giving spare plants and 'Collections' may be bought cheaply, but soon the owner will begin to discriminate and want special types. The cheapest way of forming a collection is by the purchase of seeds and the rarest varieties can now be obtained at a price within the reach of everyone. This method is slow, but extremely interesting.

Sooner or later the beginner will be purchasing plants from dealers. These may be either established, that is rooted plants, or recently imported, unrooted plants. If he covets a plant exhibited for sale at the Cactus Society's Show or at the R.H.S. Fortnightly Show, then let him give his order for delivery *when rooted.* The reasons for this are fairly obvious; cacti are collected often hundreds of miles inland in South and Central America. The roots are damaged in the process of being dug up or too often hacked up; then in addition to the journey to the coast, they have a long sea voyage before they reach this country. Any roots that may be left are useless and must be cut away. Cacti will stand a good deal of rough handling, but many of the plants are old and the older they are the longer they will take to send out new roots. A young healthy plant which is received during the summer and potted up should send out roots in a month or less, but an old one may take two years. Until it is rooted it needs very careful treatment and, unless one is prepared to take one's chance of success or failure, it is better to leave the plant in more experienced hands for a time. It is disheartening to pay a good sum of money for a valuable plant to discover after six months that it is dead.

If signs of decay are discovered, a plant may still be saved by cutting away all soft or discoloured portions and drying off the cut portions and replanting. If the plant is an old one, it possesses but little vitality and the chances are against it re-rooting, though it may be possible to make it grow by grafting on a suitable stock.

A question which the beginner may well ask himself quite early in his career as a collector is whether he intends to specialise or just acquire every cactaceous plant that he can secure. This is not a question which anyone can decide for another because tastes differ so much. But one consideration may be pointed out. If you are going to callect indiscriminately, unless you are an individual of considerable leisure and means, you are not likely to acquire a really representative collection; whereas if you limit your collection to certain genera, you have a chance of getting together something really good.

It may be that certain cacti make a greater appeal to you than others. You may have a fancy for the Cereus and its allied forms, Cereanae, as Britton and Rose call them. This sub-tribe contains many beautiful kinds including the hairy *Cephalocereus senilis*; there are thirty-nine genera in all. Or you may admire the Mammillarias, which with thirteen other genera, make up the sub-tribe Coryphanthanae. Or again the Echinocactanae, with its twenty-eight genera.

Once the initial enthusiasm for the quickly succulents

has been satisfied by a more or less indiscriminate collecting, there is nothing that will keep the collector's ardour so keen as concentration. There are many collectors who simply cannot resist a new plant, and we deeply sympathise with the feeling, but if in addition to your love for all cacti you add an ambition to secure a better collection than anyone else of a particular group, it certainly adds a stimulus by giving you a definite goal to aim at. All cacti are worth collecting. If any discrimination is made it might be made against the tall growing Opuntias, which take up a lot of room, and are so easy to grow that the pride of possession is thereby lessened. This does not by any means apply to all the plants in the genus; there are some quite attractive species.

The names of a few plants suitable to begin with are given below, but it is generally safe to buy any well-rooted plant that appeals, unless warned by the dealer that any special difficulty attaches to its cultivation. The brief descriptions attached to each are intended to give some idea of the general appearance of the plant and not for purposes of identification.

OPUNTIA

O. basilaris. A low growing type, not very spiny, the joints bluish or tinged with red.

O. bergeriana. A tall growing plant with bright green joints and long spines. Old plants flower freely.

O. cylindrica. The stem is cylindrical instead of flattened and has a few white spines.

O. imbricata. Another cylindrical type with many whitish spines.

O. leptocaulis. The stem is cylindrical and quite thin but branches freely; the few spines are very long.

O. leucotricha. This has flat joints and, instead of sharp spines, numerous long white bristles up to three inches long.

O. microdasys. A species with small, pale green, flat joints; there are no spines but each areole has a tuft of golden glochids (barbed bristles). This plant should be handled carefully as the glochids come out very easily.

O. rafinesquei. A type with very large, flat green joints and few spines.

O. ursina. Sometimes known as the Grizzly Bear on account of the long grey hairs on the flat-jointed stems.

CEREANAE

Aporocactus flagelliformis. The Rat's Tail cactus has long, slender, very spiny stems; it has beautiful flowers, about three inches long, bright magenta. It is usually grown suspended from the roof and likes moister conditions than most cacti.

Cephalocereus senilis. The Old Man cactus is found in most collections. It is covered with long white hairs or rather bristles; seedlings are particularly attractive.

Cereus azureus. A slender, columnar type with about six ribs with short spines; the young growth being blue owing to a covering of wax.

Cereus coerulescens. A stout columnar form, bluish on the young growth, with short black spines. This plant is rather variable.

Cereus jamacaru. A columnar type which forms a tree 30 ft. high. Seedlings or small cuttings are very attractive on account of the bluish colour and the golden spines.

Cereus peruvianus. A columnar Cereus resembling *C. azeureus.* It was described in 1623 but, despite its name, does not occur in Peru; it is found on the eastern side of South America.

Chamaecereus silvestrii. A small creeping type which has lovely orange flowers over two inches across; the side shoots break off very easily and can be rooted. It needs a good deal of water when growing and should be kept cool and dry in winter.

Cleistocactus strausii. A beautiful columnar cactus, whose stems are almost covered by the fine white spines.

Marginatocereus marginatus. A greyish green Cereus with a stout stem; the areoles are very close, almost joined together with very stout, short spines.

Myrtillocactus geometrizans. A tree in its native place; the stems are 4–6 inches across, and the six ribs are sharp. The spines are quite short but thick. A handsome species but unlikely to flower in Britain (Pl. I).

Nyctocereus serpentinus. A climbing type with ten or more ribs and fairly long, needle-like spines. When old enough it bears beautiful large white flowers which open at night.

Trichocereus candicans. A columnar Cereus which branches from the base, stems stout, green, with about eleven low ribs and thin spines.

Trichocereus spachianus. A slender columnar cactus with thin amber-coloured spines on its many ribs. This plant is much used as a grafting stock.

ECHINOCEREUS

E. delaetii. This much resembles *C. senilis* and is sometimes called the Old Man cactus too; it never grows tall, however, and may branch from the base.

E. chloranthus. An oval cactus almost entirely covered with sharp spines. The flowers are small and yellowish green.

E. dasyacanthus. A short cylindrical type which branches

Photo by R. Gorbold

Fig. 8. ECHINOPSIS EYRIESII

from the base; the spines, reddish at first, becoming grey later, are closely pressed against the plant body. The flowers are large and yellow.

E. pectinatus. A similar type to the above, but seldom branching; the spines spread out on each side of the elongated areoles and are whitish or pink. The flowers are a deep rose pink.

E. procumbens. A prostrate form which branches freely. There are about five ribs and the areoles are a fair distance apart. The flowers are carmine.

E. stramineus. An egg-shaped plant which grows in large groups; the numerous long spines are straw-coloured; the flowers are purple.

E. viridiflorous. A small type resembling *E. chloranthus*, and also with green flowers.

ECHINOPSIS

E. aurea. A spherical small cactus with beautiful yellow flowers. This plant was discovered in 1922.

E. eyriesii. A very popular Echinopsis which has been much hybridised and the true type is not often found now. The flowers are very large, white and with very long tubes. (See Fig. 8.)

E. multiplex. A type which makes a large number of offsets. The flowers are very large and pink.

E. tubiflora. A type which grows rather taller than most Echinopsis but with the usual large flower, white inside and the outer petals with a green stripe.

ECHINOCACTANEAE

Astrophytum myriostigma. The Bishop's Cap is a very striking cactus; it has five (occasionally four or six) sharp ribs but there are no spines; the surface is covered with minute white flecks. The large flowers, which appear from the centre are pale yellow, the petals being silky in texture (Pl. III).

Echinocactus grusonii. One of the best-known plants in this group. In its native country it may reach 4 ft. in height and 2 ft. in breadth. The young plants are very attractive being covered with curved, golden spines.

Echinocactus ingens. A spherical cactus with a very woolly crown; the straight brown spines are very fierce.

Ferocactus corniger. A grey-green, hemispherical cactus with many low ribs and strong spines, some hooked. This plant becomes very large in its native habitat.

Ferocatus electracanthus. A spherical cactus with sharp ribs and bright yellow, curved spines in the areoles which are some distance apart.

Gymnocalycium multiflorus. A blue-green hemispherical cactus with strong curved spines at intervals along the low ribs. The flowers are large and pinkish with a short tube. There are several varieties.

Gymnocalycium saglionis. A blue-green cactus rather like *G. multiflorus* but the flowers are generally white.

Hamatacanthus setispinus. A low growing cactus with sharp angles and brown spines. The flowers have yellow petals and are orange in the centre; they are freely produced even on young plants.

Notocactus leninghausii. A beautiful Echinocactus which, unlike most of the plants in this genus, may become columnar; the ribs are very numerous and the plant covered with weak bright yellow spines. The flowers are yellow, last several days and do not close at night.

Notocactus ottonis. A low spherical green cactus with thin yellow spines; the bright yellow flowers, which remain open for several days, appear from the centre. This species grows well and even young plants will flower (P. II).

Notocactus pampeanus. A dark green plant with the ribs divided into tubercles and with numerous dark, stiff spines. It flowers freely, the petals being yellow with a purple stripe.

Rebutia minuscula. A small green plant with low tubercles arranged spirally; the scarlet flowers are very freely produced. It grows readily from seed and flowers when two or three years old.

Thelocactus bicolor. A spherical or oval cactus with many spines; it is rather variable in form and colour. The flowers are large, violet purple and produced on quite young plants.

MAMMILLARIA

M. bombycina. A round or cylindrical plant with a woolly crown; the spines are white and closely surround the plant whilst the central spines are reddish and hooked. The flowers are small and carmine and the fruit white.

M. candida. A beautiful low growing type covered with white spines; the flowers are small and pink.

M. elegans. A cylindrical cactus, sunken and woolly at the crown; the tubercles are arranged very closely in perfect spirals and each bears a star of small spines, with one large central spine. The flowers are carmine, borne in a ring round the top.

M. elongata. A small cylindrical plant which branches freely. There are a number of different varieties with different coloured spines; *var. stella aurata* has golden spines. The flowers are white.

M. gracilis. Sometimes called *M. fragilis*, this is a small club-shaped plant covered with short white spines, which makes numerous offsets near the top; these break off at a touch and root easily.

M. hahniana. A short, cylindrical plant entirely covered

Photo by R. Gorbold

Fig. 9. MAMMILLARIA WILDII.

with long white hairs; this is a beautiful species which has not long been known.

M. parkinsonii. A low growing species which tends to become double-headed; the spines are white and there is abundant white wool in the axils. The flowers are small and yellow.

M. plumosa. A very attractive small plant; the spines instead of being sharp are branched and soft, the whole plant looking like a feathery ball.

M. prolifera. A very small plant which makes offsets freely and soon forms cushions. The flowers are inconspicuous but are followed by scarlet fruit.

M. rhodantha. A spherical cactus with the tubercles arranged very symmetrically, the spines are slender and white or yellow; there are a number of varieties of this species.

M. schelhasei. A dark green cactus which branches freely from the base; the central spines are hooked, the numerous radial ones are soft and silky. The flowers are small, yellowish with a red stripe.

M. spinosissima. A cylindrical type with the tubercles very regularly arranged; the long thin spines, more like bristles, are chestnut brown at first becoming paler with age, but the colour varies in the different forms.

M. wildii. A small growing, elongated type which branches freely, dark green with a few thin spines. The flowers are very freely produced and are small and whitish (see Fig. 9).

EPIPHYLLUM

The true species of this genus are not grown so much as the hybrids, of which there is an endless range with very beautiful flowers in variety of colours.

CHAPTER 10

INSECT PESTS

INSECT pests that attack cacti are fortunately not numerous. Mealy bug is the worst and it would be a rare collection that was entirely free of it; but it can and must be kept within bounds. A fine knitting needle or a pair of tweezers make useful weapons for picking out the insect from the base of the spines.

Mealy bug is a small white creature that looks like a tiny wood louse; sometimes it covers itself with waxy wool, within which it lays its eggs, so that it is sometimes difficult to distinguish from the wool of the plant. A drop of methylated spirit will kill the bug and the eggs; care must be taken not to damage the skin of the plant with the needle. If the plant is badly infected, it may be sprayed with spirit or an insecticide such as Nicotine or Volck; or an insecticide in powder form can be blown in.

A form of mealy bug attacks the plant under the soil, especially the roots, where it makes white waxy patches. If a plant seems to be making no progress, more particularly in early summer, when new growth should be showing, take it out of the pot and examine the roots; if there are signs of root bug, place the plant under a tap and wash away every particle of soil. It will be found that the waxy covering makes the bug very resistant to water, but a constant stream with the help of a soft tooth brush, will soon remove the pest. When the roots are clean, remove any broken or dead ones with a pair of scissors; allow the plant to dry before placing it in a clean pot with fresh soil.

Red spider is apt to attack succulents as it flourishes in a dry atmosphere such as is necessary to the cultivation of these plants; it can generally be got rid of by brushing the affected part with water, but if this does not prove effective, a solution of Volck will soon cause the insects to disappear. They should be looked for at the growing tips of plants; the actual insect is very minute but its presence can generally be detected by the light marks caused by the puncturing of leaf or stem; in really bad cases a very fine web may be formed.

Scale is not a common pest. The best method of dealing with it is by hand picking, using a forceps or the blade of a pocket knife. Insecticides are of little use as the insects are protected by their 'scales', but washing with fairly hot water has been found an effective remedy. Plants should be examined periodically for the groups of small, light brown, circular scales for, if the pest once gets a good hold in a collection, it may be a long and troublesome job to eradicate it.

Wood lice sometimes make their appearance in old greenhouses; more particularly if the wood of the staging has become decayed or if wooden boxes are used for seedlings. They may inflict extensive damage among seedlings and around the necks of the smooth coated plants. They should be searched for and killed or may be trapped by means of the various baits recommended in the horticultural press. The use of perforated zinc for covering the drainage hole as described in the chapter on soil and potting, effectively prevents the entrance from below of any insect as large as a wood louse.

CHAPTER 11

SUCCULENTS OTHER THAN CACTI: MINIATURE GARDENS

It is very unusual for a beginner in this interesting hobby to collect only the true cacti; for one thing, he may not be able to distinguish his plants at first, and also the small collections offered by dealers generally contain both cacti and succulent plants as well. So it may be useful to add a few brief notes on some of the other succulents which a beginner is likely to acquire and may reasonably expect to keep in a healthy condition. In the course of time, it may be that the owner finds he has a preference for some special type of succulent and then he will need a more advanced book than this pretends to be.

In general the treatment of succulents should be similar to that already suggested for cacti; the fact that they are fleshy either in stem or leaf means that they normally grow in places where water is scarce. As a rule, however, they may be given rather more water than cacti and even in the resting period should not be dried out entirely. It is usually advisable to add peat to the soil as well as loam, sand and broken brick, as before; lime may always be added unless the plant is definitely known to dislike it, as it tends to keep the soil sweet.

Haworthias and Gasterias, which somewhat resemble small Aloes, are attractive little plants and present no special difficulties to the beginner. The Haworthias usually have their leaves arranged in a rosette; the edges may be toothed and the surface variously marked with spots or raised dots; in the Gasterias, the leaves are also patterned but they are arranged in two rows, not in a rosette.

One of the most interesting groups are the Euphorbias; there are some shrubby types with angular green stems set with spines, which generally grow quite easily, but the types which are most adapted to the very dry places where they are found in South Africa are quite dwarf, with columnar and even, as in the case of *E. obesa*, spherical stems; only a few species have leaves and these soon drop off. It is fairly safe to say that the more advanced the adaptation of the plant to its environment, so much the more difficult is its successful cultivation in this country; thus the shrubby types present little difficulty but *E. obesa* must be treated, like the aristocrat it is, with the greatest deference.

There are most interesting plants amongst the Mesembryanthemums; shrubby forms, with their daisy-like flowers opening to the sunshine, are becoming more and more familiar for they are largely used in planting the cliff gardens in seaside towns, where they do well. But in a greenhouse – and they need protection from frost – these plants tend to become lanky, and so most collectors prefer the smaller growing types, many of which so closely resemble the rocks and stones amongst which they grow that they are called 'mimicry plants'. The Lithops or Pebble Plants and the Conophytums are so much reduced that each pair of leaves is fused together to form a small top-shaped body with a slit across the top through which the flower emerges; the new pair of leaves develops within the old pair and at right angles to them and derive their nourishment from them until the old pair are reduced to a dry skin. In growing these plants the resting period after flowering is of importance; they should be kept completely dry from November or December, when the outer covering is beginning to lose its colour and dry up, and should have no water at all until the following year. Conophytums can have their first watering in late May or early June, Lithops not till a week or so later. Give each pot a thorough soaking by standing it in water, but do not water again until signs of growth appear, then water more frequently. In both these kinds of mimicry plant the pair of leaves will be found to have split into two if the plant has flowered. Conophytums make little clumps in a few years; Lithops are generally slower to increase. They should always be given as sunny a position as possible.

The resting period of other Mesembryanthemums varies according to the part of South Africa from which they come.

Plants which always attract attention when in flower are the Carrion Flowers or Stapelias; the flowers are generally of a lurid purple marked with yellow and they smell like putrid meat or fish, thus attracting blow flies to assist in their pollination. The plants may be recognised by their square greenish stems about half to one inch or more across; they grow fairly easily but great care must be taken with the watering, especially when they are not actively growing; they are best kept quite dry during the winter.

Other succulent plants include Crassulas, Cotyledons and Echeverias; these are mostly grown for the beauty of their leaves as many of the plants do not flower till they are a good size. The Echeverias especially have wonderfully coloured, fleshy leaves; *E. metallica* is almost iridescent and in some species the leaves are covered with a coating of wax so that they look as if they had been powdered. In these cases the surface is very delicate and if the plants are to be kept in perfect condition they must be handled with great care as the least touch or drop of water will spoil the waxy surface.

Miniature gardens or bowls planted with several different kinds of succulent plant can be very attractive and are not difficult to keep in good condition. At one time it was thought that drainage holes in the receptacle to be used were essential but experience has shown that this is not so, provided a good layer of drainage material is put at the bottom and the soil is porous. A few pieces of rock can be introduced to vary the level of the surface and will add to the decorative effect. One or two of the taller cacti with low-growing or rosette plants round them can look very decorative. If any of the plants tend to outgrow their space they can be removed and others substituted. Carefully tended and not over-watered, such a bowl can be kept in good condition for at least three or four years.

Photo by H. T. Marrable

Fig. 10. A Group of Succulent Plants.

CHAPTER 12

SUMMARY OF OPERATIONS

THE cultivation of cacti presents no special difficulties but since their treatment varies somewhat from that adopted for plants of more normal form, it may be useful to review briefly the work to be done at different seasons.

SPRING. During March and April, most cacti will be showing signs of renewed growth; this may be encouraged by watering them a little; a fine dry day should be chosen and the watering done in the morning. Twice or three times during March and once a week during April will probably be sufficient. Any repotting that is required may be carried out now and all pots should be examined when first watered to see that the drainage is good. Any plant that does not appear healthy should certainly be turned out for examination and repotted. Air should be given freely on every fine day; in fact, the ventilators should only be closed in the daytime during fog or very severe frost. Artificial heating may be discontinued when the night temperatures do not drop below 45°F. (7°C.).

SUMMER. During the summer months cacti are growing actively and require plenty of water, provided that it drains through quickly. They can be watered every day but the supply should be reduced if a period of dull, cool weather occurs. In very hot weather it is best to water in the evening for there is less risk of damage if drops remain on the plants, as these will have dried up by morning. Spraying on hot evenings is very beneficial and also helps to clean the plants. A watch should be kept for red spider which is apt to develop in a hot, dry atmosphere.

AUTUMN. Towards the end of August, the amount of water given should be reduced so as to ripen the plants; in September, once a week will be sufficient and most cacti can be completely dried off by the end of October. The Epiphyllums are the chief exception; these plants should have a little water all through the winter; in fact, they do better in rather moister conditions than the majority of cacti. Mealy bug is apt to make its appearance and should be kept under control; if there are only a few, hand picking is best; sometimes they infest plants whose spines are so closely pressed against the plant that the insects cannot be removed without damaging the spines, then spraying with an insecticide will probably be sufficient, but in bad cases the plant may be removed from its pot, soaked in insecticide for an hour or so and then repotted. Heating must be begun as soon as the night temperature drops below 45°F. (7°C.).

WINTER. During the winter months, from the end of October to the beginning of March, the majority of cacti need no water. The plants should be examined periodically and if any show serious signs of shrivelling, they may be watered once; Opuntias are the most likely to need this. If the plants are quiescent, the owner need not be; this is a good time to overhaul labels, see that they are clean and legible. If a list of the plants is kept, this may be checked against the plants to see that it is correct. The pots may be cleaned and the staging also, but painting and repairs to the house are best deferred till warmer weather, when the plants can be put outside temporarily. During this period, ventilation should be given during the daytime whenever possible, probably every day except during fog or very severe frost. The heating will have to be kept going continuously but should never be forced; plants dislike the dry air produced by overheated pipes and, provided the frost is excluded, it is better to let the temperature fall a little rather than maintain it at too high a level.

INDEX